YOUTH BASEBALL

A Coach's and Parent's Guide

Wendell Kim
Sally Tippett Rains

COACHES
CHOICE

ISBN: 1-57167-097-1
Library of Congress Catalog Card Number: 96-71930

Book Layout: Michelle Summers
Cover Design: Deborah M. Bellaire
Diagrams: Terry Gieseke

Coaches Choice Books is a division of: Sagamore Publishing, Inc.
                                                P.O. Box 647
                                                Champaign, IL 61824-0647
                                                Web Site: http//www.sagamorepub.com

DEDICATION

This book is dedicated to all of the youth leaguers who love to play baseball, and to their parents, who spend a lot of time supporting their ballplayers, by driving them to practice, watching games or coaching. It is also dedicated to the older players who have stuck with the game and continue to work hard every day. If you work hard, you can achieve great things.

Wendell Kim

I dedicate this book to Bill Wilkerson, Warren Powers and the late Robert Hyland who helped a young journalism student find a place in sports as a person and not a female sports reporter, a long time ago. I would also like to thank Wendell Kim for all of his work on this book.

Sally Tippett Rains

CONTENTS

Each spring my family and I look forward to that date in February when the pitchers and catchers report to spring training. It seems that no matter how cold it is outside, just knowing it is almost baseball season warms us up and excites us. When we moved to Arizona it was a dream come true, because here they play baseball year-round.

It was in Scottsdale, where the San Francisco Giants train, that we took our sons to a baseball clinic, and I had the pleasure of hearing Wendell Kim speak. He is very enthusiastic and knowledgeable about baseball, but what I liked best was his practical advice.

My husband, Rob, has always coached our sons' teams, and I have enjoyed helping. We have spent a small fortune trying to make sure the boys get whatever they need to play.

Wendell said sensible things like, "You don't need to spend a lot of money on baseball equipment when you are starting out." He talked about picking up balls at garage sales, and making your own batting tees. As I listened to him, I thought, "This is really good information that I think other parents would like to hear." I approached him about putting it all down in a book, and he agreed to do it.

It is our hope that this book contains a lot of information that is valuable to you, as youth league parents, coaches or players. The more you know about baseball, the more fun it will be. Hopefully, you will be so enthusiastic you will run out to your position every inning like Wendell Kim runs out to his position as third base coach for the Boston Red Sox.

S. T. R.

PREFACE

Watching Major Leaguers perform at the top of their ability makes the game of baseball seem so simple. In reality, it's hard to hit a baseball. It is perhaps the hardest task to perform in any sport.

Throwing and catching a baseball also looks easy, but in reality, those skills are also hard to master. Major Leaguers who make it look so easy do so not only because of raw physical ability, but because they have been practicing those skills on almost a daily basis for all of their lives.

Those players had help along the way, from parents, coaches, and friends, people who gave them suggestions and tips that helped them improve their game and refine their skills.

This book has the same purpose. It is not designed to make every boy or girl a Major League prospect, but it is designed to provide tips and information that will make the game of baseball more enjoyable.

Playing baseball well is a great feeling. Hitting a home run or making a diving catch gives youths as well as Major Leaguers a warm feeling of accomplishment. However, the game of baseball is built almost more on failure than on success. Even the best hitters in the game make seven outs in every ten at-bats. Learning how to deal with that disappointment, and not crushed by it, is one of the keys to success in baseball or in any sport.

Using the drills and other ideas and suggestions in this book should help youths have a better understanding and appreciation of the game, and should make them understand even more why they got a hit or why they struck out.

The most important ingredient to success and enjoyment in baseball is just to play. Players and coaches can both read this book, use the information provided and the tips and suggestions about how to make a batting tee or a batting net, then go out in the yard and practice, practice, practice.

Baseball is a great game, and using the knowledge and information in this book will make it a more enjoyable experience.

W. K.

CHAPTER 1

Baseball is a Great Game

Even though the game of baseball has been called "America's Pastime" and "The Great American Game," it is becoming increasingly popular around the world. With Major League Baseball International setting up federations in many countries, more and more people are learning about baseball.

For newcomers, a quick rundown on how to play the game is easily provided. A game involves two teams, the team "at bat" and the team "in the field." The object of the game is for the team at bat to hit the ball, and the team in the field to catch the ball.

A player hits the ball that is thrown to him or her by the "pitcher." There are four bases arranged in a "diamond" shape (first base, second base, third base and home plate). After the ball is in play, the batter (who was standing at home plate) runs to first base (thus becoming "the runner"), then runs to second base, to third base and then back to home plate. If the runner makes it back to home plate, a "run" is scored. The team that has scored the most runs after nine innings is the winner.

At least three players will have a chance to hit (bat) each inning, because there are three "outs" per inning. An inning is complete when both teams have made three outs. The teams trade places after every three outs.

There Have to be Rules
The game of baseball is basically a simple one; the idea is the same in the youth leagues as it is in the Major Leagues. Youth leagues may have slightly different rules. For instance, there are nine innings in the Major Leagues, but maybe only six or seven in youth leagues depending on the organization. In the Major Leagues, the bases are 90 feet apart, but the distances are much shorter when the players are younger. The same goes for the pitcher's mound. In the Major Leagues, the mound is 60 feet, six inches from home plate. A youth leaguer would have trouble getting the ball over the plate from that distance.

Playing Smart
Even though baseball is a lot of fun, it can sometimes be a dangerous game. As a result, players need to be sure to play both smart and safe. During the game, the players on offense (i.e., at bat) use wooden or aluminum bats. Because at any given

time, baseballs or bats could be flying during practices or a game, parents should encourage younger players to be sure to use batting helmets any time they are up to bat. Catchers should be adequately protected with a face mask and chin strap, chest protector, knee pads, and for the boys, an athletic supporter.

Whether playing sandlot baseball or Major League baseball, players should remember to have fun and take care of their bodies. They should do some stretching before they play so they will not pull any muscles. The players should try to eat right and stay in shape. Younger players, especially, should not abuse their bodies (i.e., use alcohol or drugs) if they want to be good baseball players. I used to tell the younger players that if they took drugs they would not be able to play baseball. Unfortunately, some Major Leaguers have gotten away with using drugs. Their actions are a personal choice . . . a very bad choice. If players keep themselves fit, they will be better baseball players. Another thing players should remember is to respect their coaches for the time and effort they are putting into practice. Players should come to practice ready to play.

Which Players Have a Chance to Make it to the Big Leagues?
Everyone has a chance to play professional baseball. All my life, I have always been the shortest player on all of my baseball teams. Many people told me I would not make it because of my lack of height. Because it was my dream to make it to the Major Leagues, I worked very hard. I learned as much as possible about baseball and played baseball as much as I could.

Furthermore, I hustled everywhere on the field because I wanted to show everyone I could be a Major League player. Today, I am still hustling as the third base coach for the Boston Red Sox. Before becoming a coach, I played eight years of professional baseball with the San Francisco Giants' organization. The point to keep in mind is that there are many jobs available at the professional level. While my dream of making it to the Major Leagues came true, it has been as a coach and not as a player.

In baseball, as with everything in life, if someone wants to make it, he must be dedicated. Players should go for it and not listen to people who try to bring them down. Certain players may be slow, so they should work on their conditioning, their baseball skills, and the mental part of the game. If they are not very good at hitting, then they should concentrate on being the best defensive players they can be. Fortunately, there is room on the baseball field for all sorts of different types of people.

What about the players who really love baseball but do not have the necessary skills? They should keep their grades up in school; a good education will help in their future. Sometimes a player's career is cut short due to injury or being released; other times a person chooses a job other than playing. Some other baseball-related jobs include marketing, accounting, retail, stadium operations, ticket sales, and radio, television, or newspaper reporting.

One other possible by-product of playing baseball is the chance to earn a college education. If players work hard and become skilled at baseball, they could have an opportunity to earn a baseball scholarship. If you think you may want to go to college on a "free ride," you should make sure that you keep your grades up. Many baseball players have been disappointed because they were turned down by universities and colleges simply because their grades were too low. Players should do their homework before they go to practice (or as soon as they get home).

What Equipment is Needed?

When players first start playing baseball, they do not need to go out and buy the most expensive glove or bat. What they need most is just some equipment to learn skills with and practice. If they decide that playing baseball is something they want to continue, then they can invest in some new equipment.

There are many ways to obtain a baseball glove when someone is just starting to play the game. A player may borrow a glove from a friend or neighbor. Chances are the player knows someone who may have an old glove, and might be happy to loan it. In areas where garage sales or swap meets are held, a player might be able to pick a glove up inexpensively. Used sports equipment shops are also being established all over the United States. There is one advantage to having an old glove. It is already "broken in" (refer to section on breaking-in a glove). All factors considered, it is easier to catch with a glove that is already broken-in.

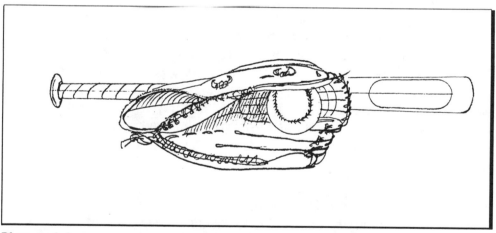

Diagram 2-1.
Used baseball equipment can be found at garage sales, swap meets or used equipment stores.

Any time players see an old ball (of any kind) that nobody wants, they should pick it up and save it. They do not just need baseballs when practicing. Whiffle balls are great for practicing hitting when a player is just starting out. Whiffle balls are also a great tool for kids who are scared of a real baseball. If they can get used to catching a whiffle ball, over time they will gradually be able to adjust to the "hardness" of a baseball by next using a rag ball, then a tennis ball and, finally, a baseball. Tennis balls are a good tool to use for practicing fielding. Players can throw a tennis ball against a wall and practice catching it. Tennis balls bounce back better than baseballs. Even those brightly-colored rag balls that little children play with are good to practice with because the bright color helps the new learner concentrate on seeing the ball better. The point to remember is that many Major Leaguers started out with less than perfect equipment.

Doesn't the Equipment Cost a Lot?

Parents do not need to spend a lot of money in the beginning of a child's baseball career. Otherwise, when players find out that baseball is not the sport for them, they wind up with a lot of baseball equipment and nothing to do with it. Another reason not to invest a lot at the beginning is that the child will grow and may need new equipment very soon. I conduct a lot of clinics, and parents always ask about equipment.

Fortunately, there are many ways to obtain equipment. For example, if necessary, other ways exist for players to make their own baseball equipment, including batting tees, catching devices, weights for bats and batting cages (refer to the section on making equipment).

Swap meets, garage sales, flea markets or rummage sales are excellent sources for equipment. If you're lucky, you might find a glove or a bat, but balls are the best item to get at a garage sale. An old baseball that is ripped can easily be taped up and used in practice. Also, if a rummage sale has baby items, you should look for baseball-sized, brightly-colored balls. They can be very valuable in trying to help a young player see the ball and stay interested in the game. Old tennis balls are also good for tossing up against a wall to practice catching. Whiffle balls and even whiffle golf balls can be helpful when learning to hit or working with someone who is afraid of the ball. Finally, another way to obtain equipment is to borrow it from friends or neighbors.

For coaches, I recommend you do what I do. If I see a ball of any kind that does not belong to anyone, I will pick it up and put it in my trunk. I keep a bag of balls with me for clinics. All factors considered, the more baseballs you have, the easier your practices will run. As you will find, almost any kind of ball can be used in practicing baseball.

CHAPTER 3

Making Your Own Equipment

Weights for Bats

"Water wings" or "floaties" can be used for bat weights. These items are often found at sales, or you may even have an old pair of your own. If used as weights for bats, they should be filled up with water or sand to the desired weight. The hole in the middle should be slipped over the bat to create a weight that will work as well as any store-bought weight. Plastic bags can also be used somewhat in the same way. For example, a plastic bag can be filled loosely with sand or water and adhered around the big end of a bat using some kind of tape.

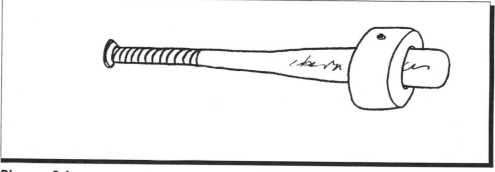

Diagram 3-1.
Weights for bats can be made by filling " water wings" up with water or sand.

The purpose of using weights is so the bat will feel lighter when the weights are removed. If players get used to swinging a heavier bat, then when they use their own bat, they will feel like they have better control of it.

Batting Tees

Batting tees can be made from some old scrap wood and a radiator hose. A radiator hose typically costs approximately five dollars. Although a radiator hose is usually the best option for making a makeshift batting tee, you do have other alternatives. For example, most hardware stores also carry rubber tubing ($1\frac{1}{2}$" diameter tubing is needed). A foot of this tubing may only cost two dollars. Because the tubing may not stand up straight, it should be put on a pole, and a hair dryer used to straighten it out. The hose or tube is really the only part where an expense will be incurred if scrap wood is available. The radiator hose or rubber tubing should extend above the pole at the top, so if the tee is hit, the bat will not hit the wood and knock over the tee. The radiator hose has "give" and will bounce back.

Portable Batting Tee

Materials:
- Wooden base (scrap plywood works well) approximately one and a half square feet.
- Approximately one foot of rubber tubing or a radiator hose (should slip over the pole)
- Wooden pole (dowel rod, will work)—1^1/$_2$" diameter
- Four 2" corner braces
- Sixteen ^{3}/$_4$" Phillips wood screws
- A saw to cut the wood to the desired size.

Directions:
- The coach should first decide how tall the batting tee needs to be. This figure can be determined by the strike zone of the person for whom it is being made. The pole should be cut a little shorter than the actual size needed.

- The wood should be cut in the shape of home plate (the design can be traced). The brackets are attached to the dowel rod with the screws and screwed into the center of the wooden base. The hose slides on the top of the rod (refer to the diagram). Once the baseball is set on top of the tee, the player is ready to hit. If the tee is too tall, the dowel rod can be cut a little. The height of the tee can be adjusted by moving the rubber tubing up or down. The batting tee is portable so it can be put away when the player is finished.

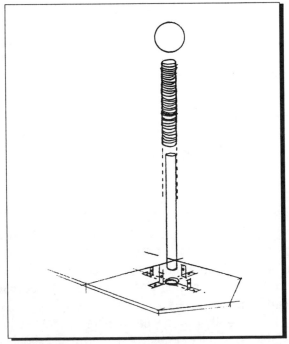

Diagram 3-2.
A portable batting tee can be made with wood and a radiator hose or other rubber tubing.

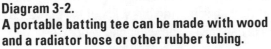

In-Ground Batting Tee
Materials:
- Approximately 12" long plastic PVC pipe
- Wooden pole or closet dowel rod ($1\frac{1}{2}$ inch diameter)
- Approximately a foot of rubber tubing (or radiator hose) with the same diameter as the wooden pole.

Directions:
- A foot-deep hole about the diameter of the pipe should be dug in the ground. The pipe should be stuck in the hole, with a little of the pipe sticking out of the ground. A piece of wood (pole) should be cut. The rubber tubing should be attached at the top of the pole. The pole with the tubing at the top should then be slipped into the pipe in the hole.
- A player is ready to practice once a ball is set on top of the tubing.
- The whole tee can be left in the ground, or the wooden rod and hose can be taken out, leaving the pipe in the hole for future use.

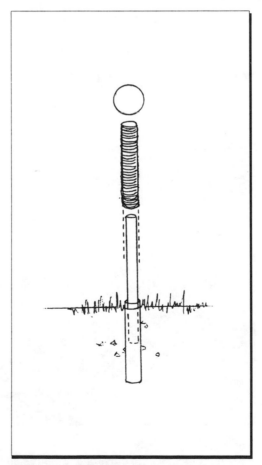

Diagram 3-3. Pipe in the ground serves as the base for the in-ground batting tee.

A Word about Batting Tees

One important point that should be remembered about tees is that they are not just for tee-ball players. Five- and six-year-old children play tee-ball before they advance to baseball. Sometimes, older players erroneously believe that using tees is no longer appropriate or beneficial. On the contrary, tees have been found to be a very important tool in developing a level swing. Accordingly, ballplayers of all ages can and should practice with tees.

Sometimes, players do not realize they are not swinging level. As a consequence every player should periodically practice with a tee. Robby Thompson was a good example of someone who did not even know he had a problem with swinging level while playing in class A minor league baseball. While I was working with him, I told him he should be swinging level. He said he thought he was, so I had a few of his teammates watch his swing. I asked him to close his eyes and swing the bat as level as possible. After Robby swung the bat, I asked the other players if he was swinging level. They all said no. Robby now plays second base for the San Francisco Giants and has become a very successful hitter. This story, however, illustrates the point that even players who go on to become Major Leaguers need to work on their swing periodically. In my coaching career, I've used tees with players of all ages in a variety of leagues.

Photo 4-4.
Batting tees can help players of all ages and abilities.

Homemade Catching Device

Materials:

- Scrap wood (approximately one foot by one foot)—sawed into a circle, or it could be used square.
- A plastic strip or doubled fabric strip about six inches long and one inch wide.
- Small nails to attach the plastic or fabric to the wood.
- A saw to cut wood into a circle if desired.

Directions:

- This flat catching device which is used to help players learn to catch with two hands can be made out of wood. The piece of wood should have a strap attached to the back.

- Players use this device to play catch the same way they would with a glove, except that a glove will hold the ball, while a catching device will not. This device makes players practice catching the ball with two hands.

- Another way to accomplish the same objective is to have a player use a very small glove that barely fits the individual's hand. If the glove is so small it barely fits, the player will have to use two hands to catch the ball.

- A commercial item currently on the market called Soft Hands is also designed to make a player catch the ball with two hands.

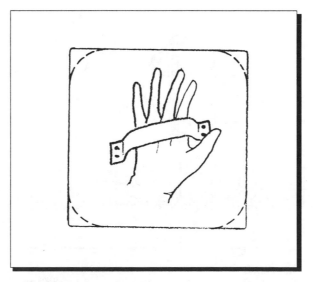

Diagram 3-4.
A homemade catching device can help a player learn to catch the ball better with two hands.

Tire Batting Practice Tool

Materials:

- A rubber tire.
- Rope to attach the tire to something (e.g., a tree, a pole, etc.).

Directions:

- A tire should be attached to a pole (or a tree) using the rope to tie it up tightly. The rope can be woven through one side of the tire, wrapped around the pole, and then woven out of the other side of the tire and repeated. The tire is hung or secured at a desired height. The players practice swinging the bat and hitting the outside of the tire. The tire will "give," so players will not hurt themselves. The tire batting practice tool can be used to build muscular stamina (strength and endurance) in the players' arms when they practice their swings. Using this device also enables players to work on swinging level.

- A piece of chalk or tape can mark the tire to give players an aiming point on the tire to hit. This practice tool is particularly useful for older players. Because it can place excessive demands on a player's arms, this tool may not be appropriate for younger players. Special care should be taken if it is used with pre-high school aged players.

Diagram 3-5.
A tire batting practice tool can be used to build muscular stamina in a player's arms.

Ball on a Rope Device

Materials:
- A baseball (preferably an old one).
- Some rope (clothesline or thinner).
- A drill to make holes in the ball.
- Two PVC pipe "L" joints with about 3" pipe sticking out (refer to the diagram on page 22).
- Approximately $3^1/_2$ feet of PVC pipe that will attach to the two joints. Coaches should determine how tall the device should be and then figure out how far they want the pipe to stick out. A bat length can be used for this calculation (the horizontal pipe) so the ball won't end up being too close to the vertical pipe. PVC pipe cutters should be used to cut the pipe (preferably at the store when the pipe is purchased).

Directions:
- A hole should be drilled through the middle of a baseball that is placed in a vice (a power drill or a regular drill can be used to drill the hole). A rope should be stuck through the hole and either tied in a large knot below the ball or pulled up and tied to the part of the rope above the ball.

- The PVC pipes should be attached to each end of the "L" joint. The rope is then slipped through the entire "L" shaped contraption. The ball is at one end of the rope.

- The coach has several options when making this device, depending on how flexible the ball-on-a-rope device needs to be. For example, a metal pipe can be used instead of PVC and stuck in the ground to add more stability. The easiest option is to just attach the contraption to a basketball goal or to some other stationary pole with a rope. One rope should be tied around the top and around the bottom to secure it in place. This method allows the device to be taken down and brought to practice. Once it is set up, the ball should be hung from a height the player wants to hit from, with the excess rope wrapped around the bottom of the pipe. Players should practice hitting with it like they would with a tee. Since it is made of PVC pipe, the device will never be completely sturdy. However, it can be a very useful tool that does not cost very much.

A ball can also be hung on a rope from a tree or some other elevated source. When using the ball-on-a-rope device, players should be very careful to get out of the way after they hit the ball so they do not get hurt.

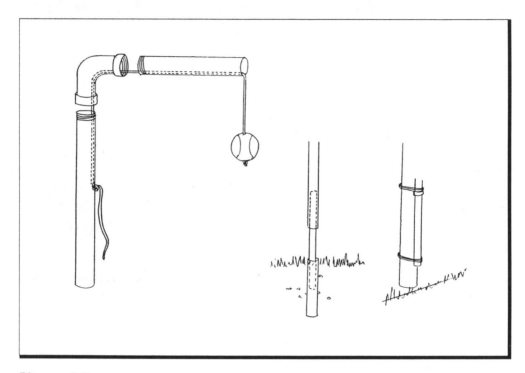

Diagram 3-6.
A ball on a rope is a good way to practice hitting when players have no one to pitch to them.

Batting Cage or Net

A simple batting net will stop balls. However, someone with the necessary resources and skills can build an effective cage to use in the backyard. A "batting cage" is a perfect place to practice pitching with a catcher even if no one is batting. A batting tee can also be used with the cage or net.

Batting Net Device

Materials:
- A baseball net. The holes in the net should not be too big; for example, a soccer net would not work.
- Clothesline or other rope.
- Something to attach the net to—trees or poles.

Directions:
- The netting can usually be obtained through a variety of sources (e.g., sporting goods stores, hardware stores, etc.).
- One approach to making a batting net device is to decide the size wanted, have a net made that size and attach ropes on each corner. The corners of the net could then be secured (for example, to two trees as shown in Diagram 3-9).
- Another method for making such a device would be to tie the net to two poles that would then be placed somewhere in a yard or on a field.
- The batting net device could also be tied to two stationary objects at the ball field (i.e., one end to the fence and another to a tree).

Diagram 3-7.
A batting net helps keep the ball from getting away during your practices.

Simple Batting Cage

Materials:

- A baseball net (refer to the discussion of materials for a batting net).
- Two-by-fours or PVC pipe for the frame. A metal pipe could also be used.
- Hammer and nails.

Directions:

- A simple batting cage can be made by assembling PVC pipe and attaching the net to the pipe (refer to the diagram below). The same cage can be built using two-by-fours. The PVC pipe option has several advantages. PVC pipe is light and can be taken apart and used at a later time. On the other hand, it would have to be secured. One alternative would be to tie the PVC cage down (a rope should be attached both to the bottom of the cage and to a tree or even tent stakes). A wooden frame or metal pipes may offer an even more sturdy option for constructing the frame.

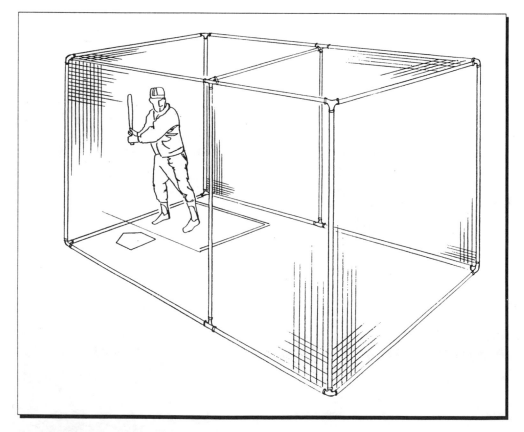

Diagram 3-8.
A batting cage made from PVC pipes would have to be anchored down by using tent stakes or some other anchor. The cage can be made of either wood or metal.

Jump Ropes

Materials:
- Commercially sold or self-made jump ropes.
- Chalk.

As a general rule, jump ropes are relatively inexpensive. Despite their low cost, they can be very useful tools to help players practice various aspects of the game. Any type of jump rope can be used. Older players often prefer the so-called heavier types of jump ropes that are typically available for purchase at most sporting goods stores.

Four Ways To Use a Jump Rope

- *Side to Side*—This movement is designed to enhance the myriad of baseball-related actions involving side-to-side movement. For example, it will help pitchers move quickly to either the left or right side to field a bunted ball. It will also help them to improve their ability to cover first base. The exercise may also have a positive impact on the quickness and agility levels required of the other position players. For example, a catcher may enhance the quickness required to block the ball to the left and right. An infielder may improve the ability to go left and right for ground balls. Outfielders may increase their ability to go after balls hit to the outfield.
- In order to perform the exercise, players should draw an imaginary line through their legs and jump over the line from side to side while facing straight ahead (refer to the diagram below).

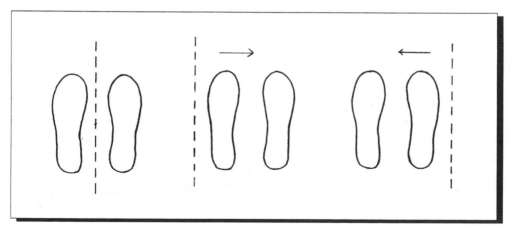

Diagram 3-9.
Side-to-side jump rope.

- *Forward and Back*—This exercise is designed to enhance the ability of a pitcher or catcher to react to bunted balls in front of home plate. It will also help infielders and outfielders to come in on ground balls and go back on fly balls. To perform the exercise, players should draw an imaginary line in front of their feet (perpendicular to their body). They should jump forward and back over the line. They should also jump up and back repeatedly (refer to the diagram below).

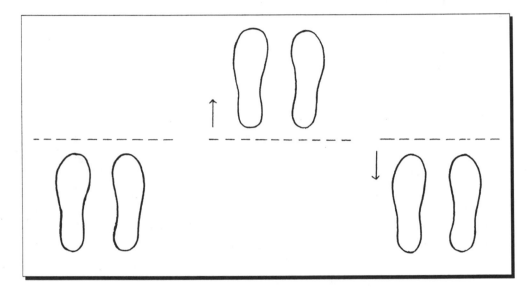

Diagram 3-10.
Forward and back jump rope.

- *Double Jump*—This exercise is a good drill for concentration. The rope should go around the player twice before his feet hit the ground. All factors considered, it is the most difficult of the four jumping exercises to do. Fortunately, as a player gets older, the double jump exercise tends to get somewhat easier to perform.

The jump rope can be a very helpful tool to enhance a player's motor skills (particularly balance and coordination). The most important period of time for a youngster in growing and developing for sports is between eight and 16 years. When some youngsters grow, they tend to lose some of their balance and coordination. Sound jump rope routines can help these individuals maintain (and in some instances, enhance) their motor skills as they grow stronger and taller.

- *Four-Square*—Chalk can be used to draw a 4-square that players can practice with, or they can draw the 4-square in their head. They should jump once, then jump diagonally backwards to the right (refer to the diagram below). The next jump should be straight ahead, while the subsequent jump should be diagonally backwards to the left. This process should be repeated for a given number of repetitions.

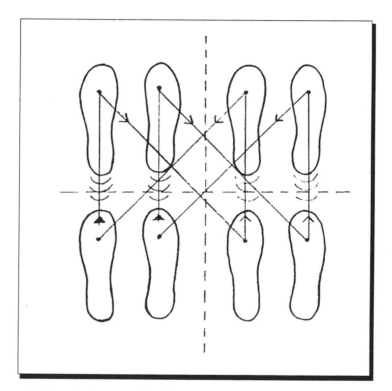

Diagram 3-11.
Four-square jump rope.

CHAPTER 4

Running a Successful Baseball Practice

Many parents volunteer to coach their child's youth league baseball team with the idea of playing the game together and having fun. In reality, they often find the practices stressful because of the additional demands on their time and energy. It is difficult enough for them to just get to the practice, let alone have the time to plan it out. When they get to practice, they may become frustrated if they feel that the youngsters are not cooperating or paying attention.

On the other hand, while children sign up for baseball for a variety of reasons, the main reason is usually to have fun with their friends. They may come to practice excited to be playing baseball, but become bored standing around waiting to take their turn at bat. The players start horsing around, the coaches lose their tempers, and suddenly the game is not as fun as it was supposed to be.

Planning It Out

Many problems can be easily avoided if the coach approaches practices in an organized manner. Before the season starts, coaches should determine how they plan to organize and run every practice. They should put this information in writing and bring it to each practice. Using the "stations" approach to running a baseball practice will make a coach's life much easier.

The same basic practice format can be used for youth leagues as well as junior high, high school, and college teams. More refinement is necessary at the professional and Major League levels, although the same basic principles apply.

Most teams will have one or two coaches; however, having a few more coaches will be helpful for the players. With young kids, if coaches can't find other adults to help, they may be able to find a high school player or two willing to help. If a team has multiple coaches, the head coach should be the organizer and tell the other coaches what they should be doing with the players.

The "stations" approach is recommended as a way to run an organized practice and use practice time efficiently. Because the team is divided into groups and each group of players is working on a specialized area, players are not standing around waiting for their turn at bat. Players spend 10-20 minutes at each station, depending on the length of the practice and how many stations are being used.

Team Meeting

At the beginning of each practice, the coaches should have a quick team meeting to discuss anything they want to tell the team and then go over the stations. It is helpful to have a drawing to show the players where each station is located. The coach should also go over how the players will rotate among the stations during practice.

A good, thorough practice typically lasts two hours. The first 15 minutes after the team meeting should be a team warm-up. The remainder of the time can be divided among the different stations and any other activities the coach has planned. It is important for the players to give the coach their complete attention at all times; a great deal of time is wasted when players are not focused on the practice. Coaches may have the team gather around and "take a knee" when they want the players' attention. If players are horsing around after practice begins, the coach may use a variety of methods to re-focus their attention (i.e., running laps, push-ups, etc.).

Players should come to practice ready to listen to the coach and follow instructions. If players develop good listening and learning habits when they are young, those habits will remain with them when they are older. All players have room for improvement, regardless of what level of baseball they play.

Diagram 4-1.
Before any practice, the coach should gather the players around for a short team meeting to let them know what will be going on at the practice, when the next game is, what is expected of them, and to discuss anything they need to work on as a team.

Team Warm-Up

The key to the team warm-up is to make it short and fun. For young players, intense warm-up or conditioning activities are unnecessary because of the children's level of activity during the day. Instead, the warm-up period can be used to focus on fundamentals. Every warm-up activity should have a specific purpose related to baseball skills.

Photo 4-2.
Warm-up.

One of the best things about an organized warm-up is that one coach (called the "special" coach) can have a clipboard and take notes. This coach should watch all of the players during the warm-up drills and write down any specific problems an individual player has. These notes will be used later in the practice.

- Running the Bases: This activity is a good way to start the warm-up. All of the players should begin at home plate and run the bases, making sure they step on each bag. This exercise will help them remember to tag the base, and it will also give the special coach time to watch for any problems the players may have in running the bases. Coaches should watch for proper running technique.

    After a few practices, colored tape can be put on the inside corners of the bases so the players will concentrate on stepping on the corners for a better turn.

    When running to first base on a ground ball in the infield, runners should run hard through the bag. They should not jump into the bag because they could hurt their leg. They should step on the front half of the base as they are going through the base with a forward body lean.

- Swinging the Bat: The players should all be given a bat and spread out on the field. The coach stands in front and throws an imaginary pitch (no ball). Everyone swings at the "pitch." The special coach also stands in front and writes down any problems players or having so those players can receive special attention in that area.

  This drill can also be performed using "hitting sticks," long, thin poles that are cut to size for each player. The players' sticks should be marked with their names. The sticks are marked with tape at the length of the player's hitting stride. Hitting sticks are also good for hand-eye coordination if used with golf whiffle balls. If players can hit a small ball with a thin stick, they have a good chance of hitting a larger ball with a bat.

- Jumping Rope (Coordination and Balance): Young players sometimes grow so fast that they lose their coordination and balance. Jumping rope is a great way for them to keep working on coordination and balance. Good balance is one of the most important tools players can have in baseball; it helps in hitting, pitching, fielding and every other aspect of the game.

  All players should have a jump rope and practice the jump rope exercises discussed in the previous chapter. If the team does not have enough jump ropes to go around, the exercises can be done during the stations portion of the practice.

- Throwing and Playing Catch: The youngsters should pair off and practice throwing and catching. After playing catch for a while, they should practice fielding ground balls. The special coach should also make observations during this time. Some players are afraid of the ball, and some do not know how to hold their glove out to catch the ball. An observant coach can spot these problems and write them down for attention later in the practice.

  In order to make the practice a little more fun, coaches can conclude the warm-up with the "Throwing and Catching Relay Game" (refer to the section on infielders).

Stations

After the warm-up, the coach should divide the team into equal groups for the stations. This process will work more efficiently if the same groups are used at each practice. This book uses a three-station method; however, depending on the number of coaches and how refined a method is desired, coaches can add their own stations.

3-Station Practice Method

Station 1—live hitting (batting practice): Group 1
Station 2—catching and fielding practice: Group 2
Station 3—special coach: Group 3

Rotation Schedule:

Group 1 will go to Station 2.
Group 2 will go to Station 3.
Group 3 will go to Station 1.

During each practice, each group will rotate to every station.

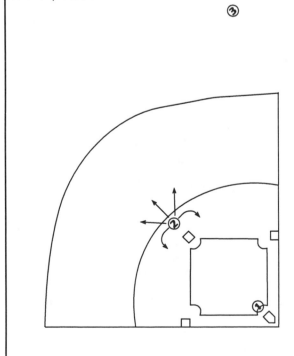

Coach's Duties:

- Set up station (equipment).
- Select each group (three groups).
- Explain what will be done at each station.
- Time each station. For example, each group should be given 20 minutes at each station. If the number of stopwatches are limited, coaches could also rotate the groups by the actions of a specific group (i.e., group 1 finishes a station, all groups move).
- Have each station last about the same amount of time. Make sure that the team does not exceed the time allotted (or available) for practice.

Live Hitting (Batting Practice): Station 1

Where: On the field.

Equipment: Baseballs (as many as possible), bats and helmets.

The coach should throw balls to the players in the group for batting practice, one player at a time. If the team has a lot of balls, the coach will not have to keep stopping to retrieve the baseballs. Each player should hit 10-15 pitches. On the last hit, the player will run the bases. The coach should tell the player, "Run on your next hit." This activity will give the players more practice running the bases.

This time should also be used to work on baserunning technique. The players should work on touching the bags properly. They should also work on their turns on the bases and on running the bases smoothly.

While the first hitter is at bat, the last hitter is working on running the bases. When the first hitter hits the last pitch, that player become the baserunner while the second hitter is hitting. Upon hitting the last pitch, the second hitter becomes the baserunner while the third hitter is batting, and so on. Each player should get anywhere from 30-50 swings during this time.

Catching and Fielding: Station 2

Where: On the field (infield and outfield).

Equipment: Fielding gloves.

The players at this station work on fielding ground balls and catching fly balls while the players at Station 1 are hitting. This group is responsible for retrieving the baseballs and giving them to the coach who is pitching. The approach will save time so the coach can accomplish more during practice.

Special Coach: Station 3

Where: Deep in the outfield, or anywhere else away from the other stations.

Equipment: Balls (all types), bats, jump ropes, gloves, and any other equipment needed to help the individual players.

The special coach station is for working on fundamentals. During the warm-up drills at the beginning of practice, this coach should have written down some notes on each player and any problems that player was having. During the station work, the special coach will be able to help the players with the areas of their game in which they need personal attention.

For example, if all of the players in the group have problems with throwing and catching, the coach can divide the group into pairs to play catch. The coach can then help correct the problems, showing the players the correct way to catch or throw the ball. The players can also work on fielding ground balls and fly balls.

If all the players in the group do not need to work on the same area, they should be divided based on the problems they are having. The coach can then circulate among the players and help them with their specific difficulties.

Additional Station Options

Coaches can adjust the number of stations used based on what they have to work with and how many players they have. Sometimes coaches will want to mix the stations up to work on other areas of the game, in order to keep practice interesting. A list of other potential stations follows.

- Tee Drill

Where: Players should hit into a net or fence, out into an open field, or up against a wall or building. If players are hitting against a wall, they should use a rag or cloth ball so it does not damage the wall or bounce back too hard and injure the player.

Equipment: Batting tee or tees and balls of any kind.

This drill is as straightforward as it sounds: the players hit the ball off a batting tee. Practicing from a tee helps players develop a level swing and helps them keep their head and eyes on the target (the ball). It can help in striding to the ball, and will also help strengthen the players' hands and arms. It is important to move the tee around so players can practice inside, outside, high and low pitches. If the tee does not move up and down, a box or a book can be put under the tee to work on the high pitch.

- Ball on a Rope

This hitting device can be used anywhere. A ball is attached to a rope so players can practice their swing, but won't have to chase after the ball. The rope should be attached to something (i.e., a strong tree branch, monkey bars, etc.) so the ball hangs about waist high. The coach should remind players to move after they hit the ball so it doesn't hit them when it comes back.

When players have no one to practice with, the ball on the rope is a good tool for them to use at home.

- Tire Drill

This drill is not recommended for players under 13 years of age. A car tire is attached to a tree, truck, fence or backstop. The player should stand in their hitting stance and take swings at the side of the tire. The coach can also make a preferred target spot on the tire. This drill is good for hand-eye coordination and strengthening the hands, arms, forearms and wrists.

- Wall Drill (Catching and Throwing)

Where: In front of a wall, building or any large vertical surface.

Equipment: Balls (tennis balls, racquetball balls).

Players should practice throwing a ball against a wall and then catching it as it bounces back. They can work on throwing to a target by throwing a circle on the wall with chalk. With a group of players, they should be spaced far enough apart that they do not interfere with each other.

Coaches may choose to set up the stations differently throughout the season. For example, at the beginning of the season, the coaches may pitch to the players. As the season progresses, the players may hit off the team's pitchers, and the coach may want to give the team more practice fielding. Coaches will discover the areas that need the most attention after the team starts playing games. They should decide how they want to run practices based on the type of help the individual players need.

After Practice Is Over

A player's baseball regimen should continue after practice is over. Players can continue working at home on the various techniques used during practice. A good way to practice baseball is by using visualization. Players should close their eyes and visualize fielding, catching and hitting. After they have visualized the process, they should practice these steps without a ball. This technique is called "shadow practice."

A mirror is another excellent practice tool. By practicing their batting stance and swing in front of a mirror, players can check their technique.

Players can also use a great deal of the equipment explained in this book at home. The tire batting practice tool, ball on a rope, and batting tee can all be used at home. If players are really serious about becoming good at baseball, they need to practice every day. It takes hard work and dedication to become a good baseball player.

CHAPTER 5

Hitting

FUNDAMENTALS

The Bat

Bats are an important piece of equipment that can make or break players at the plate. When players decide to buy a new bat, they should take their time. They should not just buy the first bat they see, or select one just because it looks good. They should select a bat they can handle.

When selecting a bat, players should make sure they swing it at least five to ten times. Hitters have a proper bat when they can start and stop that bat effectively. If young players want to buy a bat that will last them for a few years, they should buy one that is a little too heavy so they can grow into it. They can always choke up on the handle until the bat is the right weight for them to grip it at the base of the handle.

When players have several bats to choose from at practice or in a game, it is best for them not to choose a bat that is too heavy for them to handle. A heavy bat is harder to control. By the time they start playing games, players should have a bat they are comfortable with and use that bat each time.

The Grip

In the standard grip, the player aligns the middle knuckles on both hands (refer to Photo 5-1). These knuckles are the ones used to knock on a door. When players grip the bat, they should remember the word "doorknockers" to remind them of the proper grip.

When they are beginners, young players should just grip the bat the best way they can. They should do what feels comfortable. Younger players' hands are small, and it is difficult for them to worry about the proper technique when they are just starting.

As they progress, they should grip the bat correctly. The stronger hand should be on top. They should start at the bottom of the bat handle and wrap their left hand (for a right-handed batter) around the bat. The right hand grips the bat just above the left hand. Both wrists should be turned in a little to establish a comfortable grip.

Photo 5-1.
Gripping the bat.

If players are having trouble getting the bat to the ball quickly enough, they should try choking up. Choking up means taking both hands and moving them up the bat handle. The grip is exactly the same, except that it is a little higher on the bat. This technique gives players better control of the bat if it is a little too long or heavy for them.

The Stance

Several things are important when players are trying to achieve the correct batting stance. For younger players, especially, a square stance is recommended (refer to Diagram 5-2). Their feet should be about shoulder width apart, with most of their weight on the front half of the feet.

Players should be close enough to the plate that the bat reaches the outside edge of the plate. The left foot (for a right-handed hitter) should be almost even with the

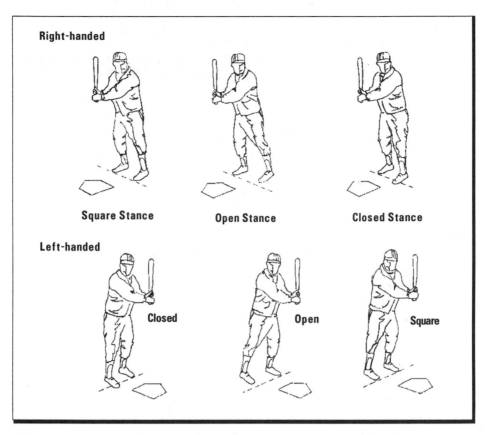

Right-handed

Square Stance   Open Stance   Closed Stance

Left-handed

Closed   Open   Square

Diagram 5-2.
The square stance is recommended. Depending on if the batter is left-handed or right-handed, the feet will vary on the open and closed stance.

front of the plate. Batters should keep their head up, with both eyes on the pitcher and their shoulders straight.

The knees should be in a slightly bent, relaxed position. The bat should be held up, and should be behind the hitter's back leg or shoulder (refer to Diagram 5-2). This position will help in shifting the weight for good position, and will allow for good balance.

As players become more experienced, they might opt for a slightly open or closed stance (Diagram 5-2). After experimenting with the slightly open and closed stances, players should use whatever works best for them.

Hands and Arms

When up to bat, players should remember to keep their back elbow up. The elbow should be just below shoulder level in a comfortable position. This position forces players to keep the bat head straight, and it gives them a more fluid swing.

On the other hand, players should not keep the elbow up too high or their swing could be a little late. When the elbow is too high, the bat head is usually pointing toward the pitcher too much, making the batter's contact with the ball late. Also, if the hands and elbow are too high, batters will automatically drop their elbow to the correct position as they begin to swing, resulting in a late swing.

Head

All parts of the body are important when swinging the bat. As the batters wait for the ball to be pitched, they should remember to keep both eyes on the pitcher. One eye is probably more dominant than the other. Batters should not lose the advantage of using their best eye in trying to watch the ball. They should turn their head a little toward the pitcher and keep both eyes on the ball from the time it leaves the pitcher's hand until it makes contact with the bat.

Bat Angle

The bat should be at such an angle that the head is behind the hitter's back leg. A good test is for batters to put the bat in the ready position and drop it. If it does not hit their shoulder or back foot, and lands a little behind them, they are in the proper position. When the bat is dropped, it should land behind the back leg. Proper bat position will help the player shift the weight enough and still allow for good balance. The hands should be about shoulder height.

Batters should try not to have the bat too high or too low. If it is too low, they have to come up on the ball. If it is too high, they will have to go down to the ball. They should keep the bat between the two, where they feel comfortable.

Stride

Batters should stride directly toward the pitcher with their lead foot. The back foot should turn on its toe, but still stay in contact with the ground, to give more power. This action is especially difficult for young ballplayers. Coaches should try telling young players to "squish the bug." This phrase gives batters something they can relate to when trying to turn their toe. Batters should concentrate on perfecting this turn as they become more experienced (refer to Diagram 5-3).

Batters must use their legs to hit. This technique is called shifting the weight. It is hard for young players to grasp what "shifting the weight" means. Beginners should not concentrate too much on the weight shift because it could hurt their timing. As players get older and more experienced, their coach or parent can help them with this aspect of hitting.

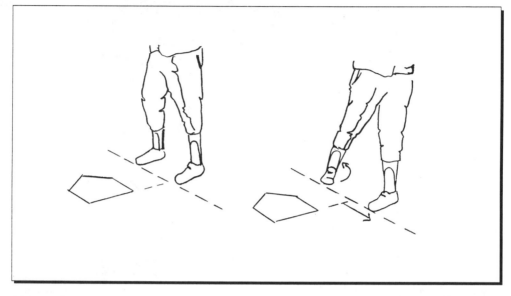

Diagram 5-3.
Batters should stride toward the pitcher with their lead foot. The back foot should turn on its toe, but still stay in contact with the ground to give more power.

By age 9 or 10, players should be working on turning that back foot to get their whole body into the swing for more power. They should work on this technique a lot in practice. Coaches can help players get their feet in proper position for the stride. Over 70 percent of youngsters will not turn their foot on their own, so the coach can lay on the ground during a batting session and turn the foot for them to give them a feel for it. Hopefully, with practice, players will not even have to think about turning their foot during a game; they will just see the ball and hit it.

Photo 5-4.
Batters should always strive for a level swing.

Swing

Batters should always strive to have a level swing. They should not try to overpower the ball or hit it over the fence. They should not uppercut or undercut. Bat speed is the most important factor in driving the ball. For this reason, it is important for batters to have a bat they can handle. If the bat is too heavy, they will have a slower swing. One of the best ways to be sure players have a bat they can handle is for them to bring their own bat to practices and games. If the team supplies the bats, players should try several of them and find the one that is right for them. For best results, players should use the same bat every time.

Follow-Through

The follow-through should include a good swing through the ball. At the end of the swing, the bat should reach the players back side. Batters should try to control their swing, not just swing haphazardly. They should dip the bat right at the end of the swing. This habit is beneficial in three ways: The swing is not cut off; no one is hurt by a thrown bat; and it is a signal to the batter that it is time to run.

If their swing is too hard, and they cannot make contact with the ball, batters should cut down the swing so they will make contact. If the swing is too hard, batters can lose their balance and fall. In addition, when players swing too hard, they often pull their head away from the ball. They need to make appropriate adjustments as they are learning to swing the bat and follow-through.

Photo 5-5.
Batters should remember to have a have a proper follow-through.

PROBLEMS WITH HITTING

If players are having problems with hitting, it may be helpful to have someone videotape them while they are hitting. The tape often reveals the cause of their problems. A video camera can be a valuable instructional aid. Sometimes batters do not realize they are doing anything wrong until they see themselves on tape. After they see the problem, or if someone points it out to them, they can begin to correct whatever they are doing wrong. Hard work and concentration are critical to becoming a good hitter. The rest of this chapter discusses problems hitters may have and ways to correct them.

The Round or Long Swing

A round or long swing is when hitters extend the hands and the bat out in a circle to the ball. This problem is also called casting the bat, and it causes the hitter to be late getting to the ball.

Holding the front elbow too high will also create a round or long swing. If the batter can keep the front elbow down, half the battle is won. One solution to help solve this problem is to put a folded towel under the front armpit to keep the elbow down until the batter swings at the ball.

Batters should not waste time casting the bat all the way around. Several drills can be used to correct a round or long swing.

- Fence Drill (Diagram 5-6): Batter should stand facing a fence, one bat-length away. Batters should take their normal swings while trying not to hit the fence with their bat (an old bat should be used for this drill). Batters should stride normally in a straight line parallel to the fence. To make sure they are striding correctly, batters can draw a line, even with their feet, parallel to the fence, and stride along this line.

Diagram 5-6.
The fence drill helps batters with their swing.

- Fence Drill with a Tee (Diagram 5-7): This drill is identical to the Fence Drill, except the batters add a tee. They should put the tee midway between the fence and their stance line, even with their front foot. As batters become more proficient at this drill, they can move the tee back toward them.

Diagram 5-7.
This drill is the same as the Fence Drill except the batter adds a tee.

- Grab the Bat Drill (Photo 5-8): A hitter holds the bat in the ready position to swing. The coach grabs the bat while standing behind the hitter, even with the hitter's body. The hitter then begins to swing. If the batter begins moving the bat out (casting), the coach can help guide the bat in the right direction.

  The Power Strap is a commercial item on the market that also helps correct the round or long swing.

Photo 5-8.
The coach tells the hitter to start the swing. Once the coach feels the hitter is moving the bat, the coach can guide the bat in the right direction.

Hitching

When batters let their hands drop as they are striding to hit the ball, it is called hitching. This problem will make the batter late in making contact with the ball.

- Bat on the Shoulder Drill (Photo 5-9): While the batters are waiting for the pitcher to throw the ball, they should lay the bat on their shoulder. When the ball is on its way and they are ready to swing, they should lift the bat a few inches off their shoulder and then swing at the ball. This drill works best in batting practice, off a tee, or during soft-toss drills.

Photo 5-9.
Batters should lay the bat on their shoulder, and when the pitcher is ready to throw, they should raise the bat up and be ready to hit.

- Holding the Shirt with the Bat in the Hand Drill (Photo 5-10): In this drill, batters begin in the ready position with the bat in their hands. They then grab their shirt with their top hand (right hand for right-handers and vice-versa), which keeps the hands in front and close to the upper body, about shoulder height.

Photo 5-10.
When batters are in ready position with the bat in their hands, they should grab their shirt with their top hand. This will keep their hands in front and close to the upper body, about shoulder height.

- Long Stick Drill: The coach has a long stick and stands or kneels behind the hitter. (The coach should not be close enough to be in the hitter's way.) Before the ball is released, the coach taps the elbow or shoulder of the hitter with the stick as a reminder not to hitch.

Photo 5-11.
If hitters are having problems with the long swing, they can practice by putting a folded towel under their armpit to keep down the front elbow until they are going to swing the bat.

Upper-Cutting

Many young players have problems with upper-cutting, or swinging upward. This problem can be corrected with a few drills using the batting tee.

- Double Tee Drill: Two tees should be placed in a line, two to three feet apart (refer to Diagram 5-12). The height of the tees will vary based on the individual hitter, but they should both be the same height. The ball should be put on the front tee. The hitter should stand halfway between the tees. The object is to swing over the back tee in order to hit the ball on the front tee. This drill will help players develop a level swing that will enable them to make better contact with the ball.

Diagram 5-12.
The Double Tee Drill helps develop a level swing.

- Tee Box Drill (Photo 5-13): This drill requires one batting tee, along with something to elevate it, such as a box, chair, or bench. The tee should be high enough that the hitter has to hit down on the ball. After trying to hit the ball on the tee from that height, the players should have some understanding of how to achieve a level swing. After a certain number of repetitions, the players should lower the tee a little and continue to hit the ball in a downward manner.

Photo 5-13.
A box should be set on the ground with a tee on top of
it to get a different height.

- High Soft-Toss Drill: In this drill, the coach tosses the batter a ball that is high enough that the hitter has to hit down on the ball. Using a rag ball or a whiffle ball in this drill is safer than using a baseball.

Overstriding

Overstriding occurs when the hitter takes a big step with the front foot. Most of the time overstriding occurs because the player starts with the feet too close together. If the feet are too close together, hitters start everything too soon and may step too far. Hitting sticks can also be used to help correct overstriding. Players should place the stick on the ground with the back end even with their back foot. They then take a correct stride and mark on the stick where their front foot should land. Players can use this tool in practice to get used to the proper distance for their feet. Some players use their bat to mark the distance they should have between their feet.

Another way to help correct overstriding or lunging is by beginning with the legs shoulder-width apart. Hitters then draw a small circle approximately six inches in front of their front foot. As they take their stride to hit the ball, they should step into the circle. If this stride feels good and the player is hitting the ball hard, then the player should use this stride when hitting. If the stride doesn't feel right and the player is not hitting the ball hard, the circle should be moved away from or closer to the front foot until it feels right.

Stepping Out or "Stepping in the Bucket"

"Stepping in the bucket" occurs when the hitter steps out away from the plate with the front foot during the stride, causing the body to turn out away from the plate. To help correct this problem, the coach can draw a line behind the players. As long as the front foot does not cross the line, the player is not stepping out. The coach may also tie a string around the hitter's front foot. As the player strides toward the pitcher, the coach can gently pull the string to keep the foot in the right position. The coach should be careful not to pull too hard, or the hitter will be thrown off balance.

Collapsing the Back Leg

This problem occurs when hitters "give up" on the back leg as they swing. A glove or a pad can be put under the hitter's back foot as a reminder to push off it and not collapse at the knee. The coach can also get behind the hitters and hold their foot so they can get the feel of pushing off. This method is often more helpful for the players.

Opening (or Not Opening) the Hips

The coach should teach players to use their hips when hitting. Sometimes they do not use their whole body weight and, as a result, fail to open their hips. For younger players this problem is not critical, but as players get older, the coach should work with them to correct this problem.

Players should turn their back foot inward. As they stride, they will feel their hips turning. This turn will provide more power from the legs. The coach should watch the front foot to make sure it is not "stepping in the bucket."

If Problems are Mental

If players are having hitting problems that are mental in nature, the coach should take the time to talk to them and encourage them. When young players are hit by a pitch, for example, they may become afraid to stand in close to the plate when batting. The coach should try to talk the players through the problem while keeping the solution as simple as possible.

If players are having trouble because they are confused by the mechanics of hitting, the coach should assure them that the primary focus should be on seeing the ball and hitting the ball. Young ballplayers should not spend too much time thinking about every aspect of their mechanics. As they get older, the coach can give them more tips, but beginners should not be given too many things to think about when they are at the plate.

A positive attitude is extremely important in baseball, for coaches as well as players. Pats on the back are an integral part of building confidence. Players cannot control whether or not a player on the other team will make a good play in the field, but they should always receive encouragement for doing their job. If a player hits a hard line drive that is caught, the coach should compliment that player on a good hit. If a player flies out, but the baserunners tagged up and advanced, the player should receive praise for moving the runners along.

Photo 5-14.
When your players are having problems which may be mental, take the time out to talk to him or her.

CHAPTER 6

Pitching

FUNDAMENTALS

The Grip

Younger pitchers should grip the ball in a way that feels good to them. Many youngsters have very small hands, and it is hard for them to hold the ball with the four-seam or two-seam grip. As they get older, they should use the four-seam grip.

- Four-Seam Grip (Photo 6-1): When gripping the baseball, pitchers should use all four seams. Using all four seams will make the ball go straight. The index and middle fingers should be placed on top of the ball, and the thumb and ring finger should be underneath the ball.

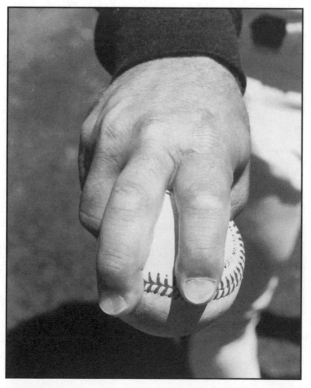

Photo 6-1.
Four-Seam grip.

- Two-Seam Grip (Photo 6-2): The fingers are placed in the same way as for the four-seam grip, but the pitcher only uses two seams. Pitchers should turn the ball to find the seams. Over the years, this process becomes automatic. Experienced pitchers do not even need to look at the ball to find the correct placement of the fingers and the seams.

As pitchers become more experienced, they should begin using the two-seam grip. Using two seams makes the ball dip and slice. If pitchers do not have good command of the ball using the four-seam grip, they should not try the two-seam grip.

Infielders, outfielders and catchers should use the four-seam grip because it makes it easier for the player on the receiving end of the throw to catch the ball. When players receive the ball, they should catch it, rub it into their hand and find the correct grip. When they are first learning, they should just throw the ball as quickly and accurately as they can. As they develop more of a feel for the ball, players should begin trying to turn the ball before they throw it.

Photo 6-2.
Two-Seam grip.

The Pitcher's Mound

When starting out, right-handed pitchers tend to stand on the right side of the mound, and left-handers tend to stand on the left side of the mound. Youth league players also tend to stand wherever no hole exists in the mound. These players need to find their place on the mound and stand there, regardless of whether the mound is torn up or another pitcher has dug a hole.

If an existing hole on the mound is not in the right place for them, the pitcher should clean it up or dig another one. This action enables them to take command of the mound and stand where they want to stand. They do not have to be governed by where the holes are.

Stepping Back

Pitchers should step back when pitching—not to the side. If pitchers step back, they will have more momentum going for them as they stride toward the hitter and release the ball. They will also have better balance if they step back than they will if they step sideways. Stepping to the side interrupts the pitcher's fluid motion to home plate.

Eventually, pitchers should be able to turn the foot that they put their weight on. They should learn to turn the foot by stepping back, not to the side. By stepping back, they will have more time to bring their arm up, and their mechanics will be better.

Hands and Arms

Beginning pitchers sometimes have problems with their glove coming up in front of their face as they step back to pitch. Pitchers who experience this problem should make sure they put their glove under their eyes or at their chin, making sure their eyes are free to see the catcher's glove and home plate.

Pitchers should also be careful not to bring their arm in front of their face as they raise their glove and the ball in the wind-up. This motion often causes young pitchers to lose their balance. Youth league coaches should be patient with these youngsters when they are learning.

Older players who have mastered balance and coordination can put their glove and arms above their head.

Head

Beginning pitchers are often easily distracted. Many youngsters take their eyes away from the catcher's glove. They should remember to keep their head facing forward, with their eyes always on the catcher's target, during the wind-up. As pitchers become more experienced, they can begin to take in other cues, but they should never take their eyes off the target for any length of time.

Balance and Planting the Pivot Foot

When pitchers step back and then stride forward, they must keep their balance so they can plant their pivot foot on the pitching rubber. For right-handers, the pivot foot is the right foot, and for left-handers, it is the left foot. This plan will help the pitcher get more push and power from the legs, putting more velocity on the pitch.

Striding and Stepping

When pitchers are ready to stride and step toward the hitter (after the pivot foot is in the correct position), the stride foot (the left foot for right-handers) will step directly to home plate. The pitcher should not kick too high or too low with the stride leg, but should instead find a comfortable, balanced position.

Arm Angle

The arm should be at a 90-degree angle when the pitcher releases the ball. This angle will help the pitcher keep the arm at the right height when the ball is released. A slightly greater or smaller angle may be acceptable for a period of time, depending on the player's age.

Releasing the Ball

Pitchers should always use a $3/4$ delivery. This delivery will be difficult for many youngsters because of their lack of strength, but the coach should have them use as close to a $3/4$ delivery as they can. As they grow older and stronger, they should be able to master the $3/4$ delivery. Pitchers should be careful not to drop their arm too low. Incorrect arm position is the cause of many shoulder and elbow injuries.

Follow-Through

Pitchers should follow-through as they push off with their back foot. When a right-handed pitcher pushes off with the right foot, the left foot will stride and hit the ground in the direction of the hitter. The right foot will then come through and land approximately even with the left foot, about shoulder width apart. This motion puts the pitcher in proper position to field the ball and make a play. Once the pitch is released, the pitcher becomes a fielder, making balance an important component of the pitching motion.

Diagram 6-3.
When releasing the ball, you should have your arm at an
a 90-degree angle, and always strive for a ³/₄ delivery.

Should Youth Leaguers Be Taught the Curve Ball?

Until approximately age 14, players should not be experimenting with throwing different pitches. Young pitchers often see Major Leaguers throwing curve balls or sliders and want to imitate their heroes. Over-eager coaches also sometimes start pitchers throwing different pitchers too early. Young players' muscles are not ready to handle the pressure or pain that can be caused by throwing curve balls or breaking balls, and experimenting with these pitches too early can damage youngsters' arms to a point where they are unable to pitch effectively.

Players should also not begin using weights until they reach high school. Youngsters can easily injure themselves by beginning to use weights too early. Coaches should encourage their young players to just enjoy the game of baseball and wait until appropriate stages of growth and development to introduce new things.

CHAPTER 7

Catching

Catchers should be players with quick reflexes and good coordination. They need to be able to react to situations quickly, because if they are not doing their job properly, a run could score. The most important skill a catcher should have is the ability to catch the ball, or at least stop it.

Beginning catchers should view their job as a game of catch. If the catcher is afraid of the ball, the coach can use a tennis ball, rag ball, rubber ball, or other soft ball during practice. As the player becomes more comfortable in the position, a regular baseball can be used. The coach should not rush into using a baseball before the player is ready.

As players get older, the catcher's position becomes more important. The catcher often has the best view of everything that is happening on the field, and should take control of situations when the need arises. On the other hand, it is also important for the pitcher to help the catcher. For example, if the ball is in a place where the catcher can not see it, the pitcher should help the catcher locate the ball. If a runner is trying to score from third and the catcher is facing away from the plate while receiving the ball, the pitcher should alert the catcher to the fact that the runner is coming home.

In high school, college, and the Major Leagues, the catcher will be responsible for calling at least some of the pitches. It is important for the pitcher and catcher to work together in this responsibility. Collectively, the catcher and pitcher are known as the "battery."

Fielding

INFIELDERS

Ready Position

When the pitcher is delivering the ball to the hitter, the infielder's knees should be slightly bent with the weight on the front half of the feet. The feet should be shoulder width apart in a square stance. The eyes should follow the ball from the pitcher to the batter. The hands should be in a relaxed position in front of the body. The glove should be slightly open and the pocket of the glove should be facing the hitter.

Many youth league and tee ball coaches have players set their hands on their thighs during the pitch. This position can be helpful because many young players have a hard time remembering how to set up as the pitch is being delivered.

Photo 8-1.
Ready position for infielders.

Footwork for Fielding a Ground Ball

When fielding, players should move toward the ball and get their body in front of it. Their body should be positioned so that the ball is coming directly at the middle of their chest. Players should make sure they are in proper fielding position as early as possible. It is better to get into fielding position a little early than too late.

As players approach a ground ball, they should step with their right foot, then left foot (they should now be in a square stance). They should reach out for the ball and bring it in toward their body. When possible, players should throw the ball using the four-seam grip for more accuracy. If the ball is hit especially hard, fielders should simply get into the ready position as quickly as possible, react, and catch the ball the best way they can.

Players should always plan to catch the ball with two hands, but they should also be aware that at times a two-handed catch is either impractical or impossible. In these cases, they should make the best one-handed catch they can.

Photo 8-2.
Fielding a ground ball.

Throwing Relay

A fun way for players to work on throwing and catching is to conduct a throwing relay. The players should form equal lines with about 10 feet between the players in line. The lines should be 15-25 feet apart.

The first player in each line should have a ball. Each line is racing against the other(s). The first person throws the ball to the second person, etc. When the ball reaches the end of the line, the last person throws it to the next to last person and so on until it returns to the front of the line.

If players miss the ball, they must throw it back to the person who threw it to them and try to catch it again. Every person must successfully catch the ball before it goes on to the next player. Players should try to catch the ball on the glove side and then turn to the glove side to make the next throw.

As players make their second throw and the ball is on its way back toward the front of the line, they sit down. The first line with all players sitting down and the ball back to the front wins.

Coaches should pay attention to the abilities of each player when dividing the players for this game. If one line clearly has better catchers than the other, the coach should mix the players around to make the lines equal. This drill should be run for the players.

Catching a Pop Fly

The footwork for infielders is very important because baseball is usually played outside, sometimes in tough weather conditions. A player's balance and coordination are important factors in making a successful catch on a very high pop fly.

Once infielders are under a pop fly they should be sure to loudly call out, "I got it" at least twice so the other infielders know to let that player handle the ball.

Once players have called for the ball, they should get in a square stance with their feet shoulder width apart. Their head should be still, with the eyes concentrating on the ball. The glove should be brought up to catch the ball, but it should not block the eyes. The knees should be slightly bent in a relaxed position, not locked, with the weight on the front half of the feet. When catching a pop fly, players should use two hands as often as possible.

After they have fielded a ground ball and are ready to make the throw to a base, right-handed fielders should step first with their right foot, then with the left, and then throw (left-handers step with the left foot, then the right, then throw). To allow for smooth footwork and to get into a good throwing position, fielders should bring the ball to their chest to find the four-seam grip as they take their two steps. Players should step in the direction they are throwing and use the proper arm angle.

OUTFIELDERS

Ready Position for Outfielders

The outfielder's ready position is basically the same as the infielder's. The knees should be slightly bent with the weight on the front half of the feet. The outfielders should also keep their eyes on the pitcher and follow the ball from the pitcher to the batter. Hands should be in a relaxed position in front of the body, with the glove slightly open.

Photo 8-3.
Ready position for outfielders.

Footwork for Fielding a Ground Ball

- Ground ball single with no one on the bases: In this situation, outfielders can be more deliberate in fielding the ground ball because they do not have to worry about throwing out runners on base. If the ball is coming toward them, fielders should move toward it and get in front of it so it is coming toward the middle of their body. An outfielder's steps before fielding a ground ball are the same as an infielder's (right foot, then left foot). The fielder should reach out for the ball, bring it into the chest, and throw it to an infielder.

  Another technique a coach can use when teaching young players is to have them put one knee on the ground when fielding the ball. In this position, they should be able to block the ball with their body even if they do not field it cleanly.

- A ground ball with a runner or runners on the bases: In this situation, outfielders have to catch the ball on the run and make a good throw to an infielder or to a base in order to stop the runner(s).

  As outfielders are coming in on a ground ball, they should adjust their foot work so they can throw the ball quickly. Right-handed outfielders should try to field the ball just in front of their left foot, with the knee bent and the right foot back (the feet should be reversed for left-handers). Players should field the ball with the glove only, bring the glove up to get in proper throwing position, and throw the ball to an infielder to stop the runner.

  If young players have trouble fielding a ground ball, they should continue to use the infielder's fielding position or the knee position.

Catching a Fly Ball

Outfielders usually have a long way to go to catch a fly ball, and may not have time to set up in the proper position to make the catch. It is most important for them to remember to keep their eyes up and run normally. They should not bring their glove up until they are ready to catch the ball.

- Fly Ball Catching Drill: A player stands approximately 15 feet in front of the coach. The coach should throw the ball high in the air at different angles to simulate a fly ball. When working with beginners, the coach may use a tennis ball instead of a baseball. As players progress, the coach may make the players run farther to make the catch.

When other players are near, outfielders should be sure to call, "I got it" when catching a fly ball. Outfielders should be balanced, concentrate on catching the ball in the middle of the glove and try to avoid blocking their vision with their glove as they raise it to make the catch. They should also use two hands to catch the ball whenever possible.

Proper Throwing Technique for Outfielders

Once outfielders have caught the ball in their glove, they should bring the ball to their chest while finding the four-seam grip and getting in proper throwing position. Like infielders, right-handed outfielders step with their right foot, then their left foot, and then throw. They should get their body into the throw as much possible.

Beginners should not spend too much time worrying about finding the four-seam grip, or they will not have time to complete the play. If players' hands are very small, they should grip the ball the best way they can to make the throw.

When to Make a One-Handed Catch

It is always better for coaches to teach players to use two hands to catch the ball. On the other hand, players should also be aware of situations when it is better to use one hand, including:

- When the player is running to the ball and it is out of reach with two hands, but catchable with one.

- When the player has to jump for the ball.

- When the player has to dive for the ball.

- When a ground ball is out of reach with two hands, but not with one.

- When players are more experienced, they can catch the ball with one hand in order to be able to throw a runner out.

Breaking in a New Glove

While making equipment or fixing up old equipment is beneficial, most players who want to play baseball for a long time decide to buy their own glove. Selecting a glove is a process that requires time and consideration. Getting a new glove is exciting; however, breaking it in will require special care. Many baseball players consider their glove to be one of their most prized possessions.

Materials Needed:
- New baseball glove.
- 1-4 baseballs.
- String, rope, or a long sock to tie the glove shut.
- Glove oil or baby oil.
- Bat, hammer, or mallet.
- Towel.

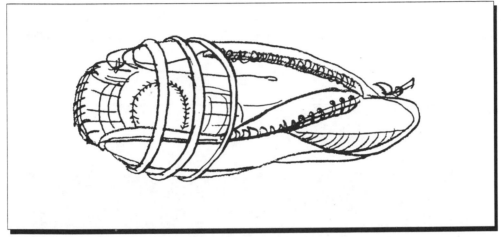

Diagram 8-4.
One way to break in a glove is to put a baseball in it and tie it closed.

Directions:
- The glove should be placed in water between 30 seconds and two minutes. After removing it from the water, the player should shape the glove and put a baseball in the pocket. The glove should then be tied shut and left in the sun to dry. Some players choose to put the ball in the glove, tie it shut, and then immerse it in water and leave it in the sun to dry.

- When the glove is dry, it should be rubbed with glove oil (available at most sporting goods stores) or baby oil. The player should then put one or more baseballs in the pocket, tie the glove shut again, and leave it to set.

- Another way to break in a new glove is to pound it with an object that will not tear it (i.e., a baseball bat, a hammer wrapped well in a towel, or a wooden mallet).

When players have spare time, they should put their glove on and throw a baseball repeatedly into it to work the leather out. Once the leather is soft, players can continue to break in the glove by playing catch. The glove can be stored with the baseballs in the pocket if it remains a little stiff.

"Flip"

Playing "flip" is a good way for players to practice using their gloves. The team stands in a circle and the players take turns "flipping" the ball out of their glove and on to the next player. Players must catch and flip the ball using only their glove, with no help from their free hand. When players miss, they turn their hat one quarter-turn. On the fourth miss, when the hat is facing forward again, the player is out. The last player left in the circle is declared the winner.

Photo 8-5.
"Flip" is a game that helps players with their catching.

Positioning Players During a Game

If coaches have an idea how the opposing batters hit the ball, they may position players accordingly in the outfield. Positioning players closer to where the ball may be hit can help the players get to the ball sooner, or even catch balls they might not have gotten to otherwise. This positioning is usually done with older players, but the coach can ask the scorekeeper to draw lines in the scorebook to demonstrate where the opponent's players hit the ball. After the game, the coach can study the scorebook to determine any patterns by individual players.

CHAPTER 9

Baserunning

Running to First Base on a Ground Ball
After hitting the ball, the batter becomes a runner. Runners should not watch the ball for very long. Instead, they should start running in a straight line to first base. They should run all the way through the base, touching the front half of the base with whichever foot they choose. That decision will usually be based on their running stride.

When the Runner Can't Take a Lead
In leagues for younger players, runners are not allowed to lead off their base when the pitcher is throwing to home plate. The player's foot must remain on the base until the pitcher releases the ball or, in some leagues, until the ball crosses the plate. The player's left foot should be on the edge of the bag closest to the next base so that the player is looking toward the pitcher and the hitting area.

When runners come off the base, they should push off with the left foot, then shuffle both feet toward the next base while watching the ball. This lead is called the secondary lead. When the ball is either hit or missed, the runner will react either by going back to their base or by running to the next base. By using the edge of the bag, the runner gains an extra step or two.

Leading Off First Base
More advanced youth leagues allow runners to lead off the bases. A very basic lead off first base is a body-length lead, which is measured from the feet to the end of the hand with the arm raised over the head. With this lead, called a primary lead, players simply "fall" back into the bag if the pitcher makes a throw to first base. When runners get more comfortable in their lead, they should be able to add one to three steps to the primary lead. Players can then take a secondary lead (as described above) during the pitch. When taking a secondary lead, runners should always be in control of their body so they can either get back to first safely or get a good jump to second base.

Photo 9-1.
Runners should remember to aim for the inside corner of the base and use that corner to push off toward the next base. They should lean a little with their left shoulder going into the turn.

Turns

Making good turns on the bases will save steps and time getting to the next base, so players should work on their turns in practice. On a sure single or possible double, players should make a gradual turn toward the outside of first base right out of the batter's box. Players who are smaller and quicker may make a smaller turn. Bigger and heavier players will need to adjust the turn, and should work in practice to determine what size turn is right for them. Players should touch the inside corner of the base and use that corner to give them an extra push toward the next base. They should lean a little with their left shoulder when going into the turn.

Tagging Up

Tagging up occurs when a fly ball has been hit to an outfielder (or possibly an infielder) and runners on base try to advance to the next base. The runners must tag the base they are on before running to the next base. Runners should be sure the ball is caught before they leave their base, and should remember to push off the base to get that extra step or two.

Remembering to Tag the Bases

Tagging the bases seems like something that should not need to be mentioned, but it is extremely important. If a player makes a great hit but forgets to tag a base, that player may be called out. Even if players think the ball will be caught, they should still run to first base. If the fielder drops the ball, batters may be able to reach first base safely if they have started to run.

On an infield single, runners may "over run" first base (touch it and then keep running for a short distance) as long as they turn toward foul territory. If they turn toward fair territory, they can be tagged out. On the other hand, runners should not turn too far into foul territory or they will have further to go to reach second base on an overthrown ball.

CHAPTER 10

Sliding

Although sliding is very important, it is often not practiced as much as other aspects of the game of baseball. Sliding feet first is recommended over sliding head first or hands first to avoid injuries.

The easiest slide to learn is the figure-four slide (Diagram 10-1). This technique is the standard slide that players have used for many years. It got its name because it looks like a figure four or a backward figure four.

How to Do the Figure-Four Slide

Player should run toward the base they are going to slide into and start their slide three to five feet away from the base. They should not slow down before they begin their slide. It is important to glide into the slide rather than jump into it. Just before they make contact with the ground, runners should pull the leg nearest the fielder who will be making the tag up into a bent position. When making contact with the ground, runners should lean back a little to take some of the pressure off their knee and ankle. They should touch the bag with the lead (extended) foot. Runners should remain on the bag until they know where the ball is.

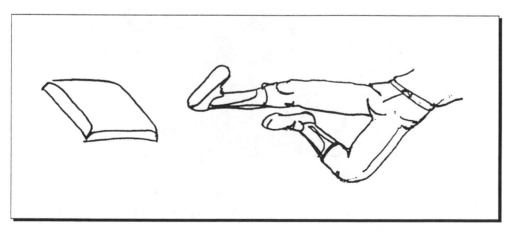

Diagram 10-1.
The figure-four side is the first slide taught in baseball. Players should remember to be safe when sliding.

Practicing Sliding

A fun and easy way to teach sliding is to have players wear their bathing suits and use a "slip and slide" or a plastic tarp sprayed with water. This method makes it easier for the players to slide, and they are less likely to injure themselves while learning.

The coach may also spray a large grassy area with water and have the players practice sliding barefoot on the slippery grass.

A third method the coach can use to help players practice sliding is to flatten large cardboard boxes (make sure any staples are removed). Players can take off their shoes and practice sliding on the cardboard in their socks.

Photo 10-2.
A good way for younger players to learn the figure-four slide is to slide on cardboard in their socks.

CHAPTER 11

Signs

When playing baseball, most younger players like to imitate the signs that Major League coaches use to tell their players what to do. A third base coach is responsible for getting this information to the batters. Youth coaches can also use signs in their games, but they should remember to make the signs easy for the players to remember. Younger players should only have three offensive signs: bunt, hit, and take.

Photo 11-1.
Signs.

Signs for Younger Players

Bunt: Belt—Whenever the coach touches the belt, the player should bunt.
Hit: Hat—Whenever the coach touches the hat, the player should swing at the pitch if it is a good one.
Take: Nose—When the coach touches the nose, the player should "take" the pitch (i.e., not swing at the ball).

Signs for Advanced Players

Indicator: Belt (The indicator signals that the player should follow the next sign given.)
Bunt: Right leg
Hit and Run: Right Chest
Steal: Left Chest
Squeeze: Left Leg
Off Sign: Face (The off sign means the plan is off. The player should not follow the previous sign.)
Take: Left Arm
Hit: Right Arm

Hitters should always look for the indicator, because the sign given immediately after the indicator is the sign they will follow. For example, according to the list above, if the coach touches the right leg, right chest, right ear, nose, belt, left chest, and hat, the sign is the steal.

Players should learn all of the signs their team is going to use. As they watch the coach give the signs, they should only look for the indicator. Once the indicator is given, they hitter should watch for the very next sign. After that sign is given, the only sign the hitter should be watching for is the off sign. If the off sign is given, the hitter should not follow the original instructions.

Coaches, parents, and players should have fun with the signs, but they should remember that keeping the signs simple will help things run more smoothly during the game.

CHAPTER 12

Game Day

Being Prepared

Coaches should remember to bring certain things to each game. Because the often have other responsibilities on game day, it is helpful to gather all the necessary equipment and items a day early.

Game Day Equipment:
- Several different bats
- Balls
- Catcher's equipment
- Batting helmets
- Scorebook and extra pencils
- Water jug

Players should be responsible for bringing their own gloves to the game. Some players will also bring their own bats. By the time games begin, the players should know which bats they are comfortable with and should have been practicing with those bats (refer to the section on selecting a bat on page ???).

Boys playing catcher should wear an athletic supporter and protective cup to help prevent serious injury. Other players (especially infielders) should also consider wearing one. In the Major Leagues, every player wears a protective cup. Coaches should talk to the catcher and their parents to be sure they are prepared for the games.

The coach should also bring a water jug so the players can have water any time they need it. They should be encouraged to bring their own water bottles, but the coach should also have water available.

First Aid Supplies

If the team is playing in a league, the coach should check with the league to see what first aid equipment is available at the ballfield during the game, as well as what procedures have been established for emergencies.

The coach should at least have ice packs available in case a player is hit by a ball or bat. The coach may bring ice in a cooler or purchase chemical cold packs. Ice helps relieve pain and keep swelling down.

An elastic bandage and a variety of adhesive bandages should also be available. It is the coach's responsibility to make sure the players have first aid available to them. All first aid supplies should be gathered before the first game.

Line-Ups

Before each game, coaches have to submit their line-up to the other team. They can decide on the line-up before arriving at the ballpark. Upon arriving for the game, they may need to make adjustments to that line-up if players are absent or late. Since line-ups must be turned in at a designated time, players who are late may not be able to start.

Coaches should encourage players to arrive early for games. Players should come to the game well-rested and physically and mentally prepared to play. If the coach has set a specific time for the team to be at the ballpark, the players should arrive on time and follow any instructions they are given. Players should always let their coach know if they will be late to or absent from a game. This effort will show the coach they are serious about their responsibility to the team.

Fit to Play

Some parts of the country have warm weather for most of the year. Players in these areas play baseball year-round. Most players, however, will spend several months unable to play baseball outside because of the weather. For this reason, the Major Leagues hold spring training for the players. They use this time to gradually work up to their regular playing form.

Many Major Leaguers have a year-round training program so they are never totally "out of shape." If youngsters are serious about baseball, they should develop their own "training program." This program can involve nearly any kind of physical activity (e.g., playing games outside with their friends, riding their bike, walking the dog, etc.) in addition to work on baseball fundamentals (e.g., catching, throwing, hitting). As players get older, they should add running and other types of physical training to their program. For young players, however, their typical amount of physical activity is usually enough exercise.

Good Nutrition

It is important for youngsters to have a balanced diet of foods that are good for them. This diet should include fruits, vegetables and dairy products. The body needs the nutrients in fruits and vegetables and the calcium in dairy products to develop properly. Parents should keep healthy snacks on hand for kids to eat instead of cookies or candy (i.e., apples, oranges, carrots, etc.). A children's multivitamin can also help provide the important nutrients the body needs.

Diagram 12-1.
Eating healthy foods helps the body develop properly and gives players the energy needed to play baseball.

In addition, players should pay close attention to what and when they eat before a game. Even if they are nervous or excited, they should be sure to eat something so they do not feel weak or get sick during the game. They should also avoid eating heavy foods within two hours of game time. Instead, they should choose lighter foods such as pasta, salad, seafood, or a sandwich. Players should also make sure they do not eat or drink too much within two hours of game time.

Scorekeeping

In league play, each team should designate a person to keep score. If a question arises about the outcome of the game, the scorebooks can be consulted. Before each game, the scorekeepers trade line-ups, and throughout the game they remain in contact with each other to supply any player substitutions or position changes. The scorekeeper's job is very important and most people are serious about keeping score for a team. Many people use pencil when keeping score in case they make a mistake. Some people also like to use several different colors for the various items they are keeping track of during the game.

Diagram 13-1. A sample scorebook page

Keeping score can be fun for both the casual fan and the youth league parent. It also helps them focus on the game the entire time. Scorebooks can be purchased at sporting goods stores. These books provide guidelines on how to keep score.

Parents who plan to be the scorekeeper for their child's youth league team will probably want to get a scorebook and learn that book's version of keeping score. The version offered here is a beginner's lesson. Different people have different ways of keeping score. For example, when a player draws a walk, some people use "W" (for "walk") while others use "BB" (for "base on balls").

People keeping score for fun should have fun and do it however they choose. Learning to keep score can help people enjoy watching a baseball game more because they are paying attention to each play and how it affects the game.

Abbreviations:

BB—base on balls/walk
1B—single
2B—double
3B—triple
HR—home run
HBP—hit by pitch
RBI—run batted in
SAC—sacrifice
SB—stolen base
PB—passed ball
WP—wild pitch
K—strikeout

Learning to Keep Score
The players' names should be written down in the order they will bat. Their uniform number and position should be included. For scorekeeping purposes, the positions are numbered as follows:

- 1—pitcher
- 2—catcher
- 3—first baseman
- 4—second baseman
- 5—third baseman
- 6—shortstop
- 7—left fielder
- 8—center fielder
- 9—right fielder

As each player completes a turn at the plate, the scorer should record what happened in the square next to that player's name under the appropriate inning using the abbreviations listed above. If a player singles, the scorer draws a diagonal line from the bottom and center of the box to the middle of the right side of the box, indicating a line from home plate to first base. "1B" is written in the center of the square. If that player advances to second base, the scorer draws a line from "first base" to the center of the top of the box ("second base"). If player had hit a triple, the scorer would have started the pencil at the imaginary home plate and drawn the line to "first base," then up to "second base" and over to "third base." "3B" would be written in the center of the box.

If the player makes an out, the nature of the out is recorded in the box. A strikeout is represented by "K." If the player hits a fly ball or line drive that is caught by a fielder, that fielder's position number is written in the box. If a player hits a ground ball and is thrown out, the numbers of the fielders involved in the play are written in the box. For example, if the shortstop fields the ball and throws the runner out at first, the scorer writes "6-3" in the box.

Sample of Part of a Scoresheet:											
No.	Player	Pos.	1	2	3	4	5	6	7	8	9
17	BJ	3	1B								
33	Dylan	9	2B								
23	Mike	4	BB								
12	Tom	2	K								
23	Bill	8	6-4-3								

In the example above, BJ led off with a single. Dylan batted second and hit a double. Mike drew a walk to load the bases. Tom struck out, and Bill hit into a double-play to end the inning.

If Mike had hit a home run, he would have been credited with three RBI (runs batted in) because he was responsible for causing three runs to score—his and the two runners ahead of him. Keeping RBI totals can help a team measure a player's true worth, because sometimes a player will make an out but still be credited with an RBI.

Pitch Count

The scorekeeper may also keep a "pitch count." Official scorebooks usually have a space to record this information by marking every time the pitcher throws a pitch.

The main reason to keep a pitch count is so pitchers do not throw too many pitches in a game. Young pitchers usually do not have very good control of their pitches and throw a lot of balls. They may throw the maximum number of pitches they are capable of in only two or three innings. If the coach leaves pitchers in a game for a specific number of innings rather than pitches, the players may injure their arms by throwing too many pitches. It is important for coaches to know how many pitches each pitcher is capable of handling so they can monitor the number of pitches and remove the players from the game if they approach their maximum pitch count.

CHAPTER 14

Awards and Congratulations for the Player

Everybody likes to be appreciated for their work. Coaches should recognize the players, and the players in turn should thank the coaches for all of the time they have devoted to the team. Parents are sometimes frustrated by the way a coach is handling their child. Unless the coach is belittling the child or otherwise creating an unhealthy atmosphere, the parents should remember that in many youth leagues, the coaches are volunteers. They are not glorified baby-sitters; rather, they are giving up their time to help children succeed in baseball and have fun, and the parents should support them.

Coaches and players alike should show support when players put forth a good effort. Simple words of encouragement can go a long way in building a player's confidence. This encouragement is especially important when players show any kind of improvement (e.g., a player who is afraid of the ball goes up to the plate and takes some good swings, but strikes out). Coaches should also remember to keep their praise specific or it may begin to lose its meaning.

Coaches should always try to emphasize the positive. If they do avoid negative feedback as much as possible, they will make playing baseball a better experience for their players.

Photos 14-1.
Whether they are a Major Leaguer or a youth leaguer, players like to be recognized for their hard work.

CHAPTER 15

Having Fun Playing Baseball

Nothing can compare to that first day back at the ballpark after a long winter. Whether it is the Major Leagues or youth leagues, baseball is a great game. It is a game that brings people together regardless of race, national origin, size, or mental capability. Baseball has a place for everyone, whether it is playing the game, sitting in the stands watching, or listening to the game on the radio at home.

Photo 15-1.
Have fun and play ball!

Baseball makes everyone feel young. An elderly man can find common ground with his grandchildren talking about baseball and sharing stories. Parents and grandparents can create family traditions by taking children to the ballpark or teaching them to play baseball.

The "boys of summer" are not just the Major Leaguers playing in the big stadiums. They are all of us—male and female, young and old—who know the love of the game. Baseball players will come and go, but the game will last forever. Those who truly love baseball will never grow old in their hearts. Play ball!

Wendell Kim is the third base coach for the Boston Red Sox. Before joining the Red Sox organization in November 1996, he served five years in a similar capacity with the San Francisco Giants. From 1989-1991, he served as the Giant's first base coach.

After playing in the San Francisco organization for eight years, Kim went on to manage at all levels in the minor leagues before joining the Giants in 1989. He has experience in coordinating the defense and infield, baserunning, and sliding instruction.

Kim is in demand as a speaker and works at many baseball clinics throughout the year. He is especially interested in helping younger players with their skills as well as with their motivation.

In the off-season, Kim lives with his wife, Natasha, and their son, Donald, in Mesa, Arizona. He enjoys performing magic and answering the many letters he receives via the Wendell Kim (WK) home page on the World Wide Web.

Sally Tippett Rains' sports background includes experience as a radio sports reporter and producer, owning a sports radio network for several years, and having articles published by *The Sporting News*.

At the time this book was written, Rains lived in Scottsdale, Arizona with her two youth leaguers, B.J. and Mike, and her husband, Rob.

Sally Tippett Rains has also co-written *Playing On His Team* with Rob Rains. (Crosstraining, 1996).